Dinosaur's Day

El día de un dinosaurio

FIRST EDITION
Project Editor Deborah Murrell; **Art Editor** Catherine Goldsmith; **US Editor** Regina Kahney;
Pre-Production Producer Nadine King; **Producer** Sara Hu; **Picture Researcher** Frances Vargo;
Picture Librarian Sally Hamilton; **Jacket Designer** Natalie Godwin;
Publishing Manager Bridget Giles; **Reading Consultant** Linda Gambrell PhD

THIS EDITION
Editorial Management by Oriel Square
Produced for DK by WonderLab Group LLC
Jennifer Emmett, Erica Green, Kate Hale, *Founders*

Editors Grace Hill Smith, Libby Romero, Michaela Weglinski; **Spanish Translation** Isabel C. Mendoza;
Photography Editors Kelley Miller, Annette Kiesow, Nicole DiMella;
Managing Editor Rachel Houghton; **Designers** Project Design Company; **Researcher** Michelle Harris;
Copy Editor Lori Merritt; **Indexer** Connie Binder; **Proofreader** Carmen Orozco, Larry Shea;
Reading Specialist Dr. Jennifer Albro; **Curriculum Specialist** Elaine Larson

Published in the United States by DK Publishing
1745 Broadway, 20th Floor, New York, NY 10019

Copyright © 2023 Dorling Kindersley Limited
DK, a Division of Penguin Random House LLC
24 25 26 10 9 8 7 6 5 4 3
003-336112-Aug/2023

A catalog record for this book
is available from the Library of Congress.
HC ISBN: 978-0-7440-8383-5
PB ISBN: 978-0-7440-8382-8

DK books are available at special discounts when purchased in bulk for sales promotions, premiums,
fundraising, or educational use. For details, contact: DK Publishing Special Markets,
1745 Broadway, 20th Floor, New York, NY 10019
SpecialSales@dk.com

Printed and bound in China

The publisher would like to thank the following for their kind permission to reproduce their images:
a=above; c=center; b=below; l=left; r=right; t=top; b/g=background
Alamy Stock Photo: Jeannie Burleson 12clb, 30cla; **Getty Images / iStock:** Warpaintcobra 12b;
Shutterstock.com: Computer Earth 4-5, 10-11, 29
Cover images: *Front:* **Dreamstime.com:** Natuska; **Getty Images / iStock:** TrishaMcmillan cr; *Back:* **Getty Images:** Sciepro cr

All other images © Dorling Kindersley
For more information see: www.dkimages.com

For the curious
www.dk.com

Dinosaur's Day

El día de un dinosaurio

Ruth Thomson

DK

Contents
Contenido

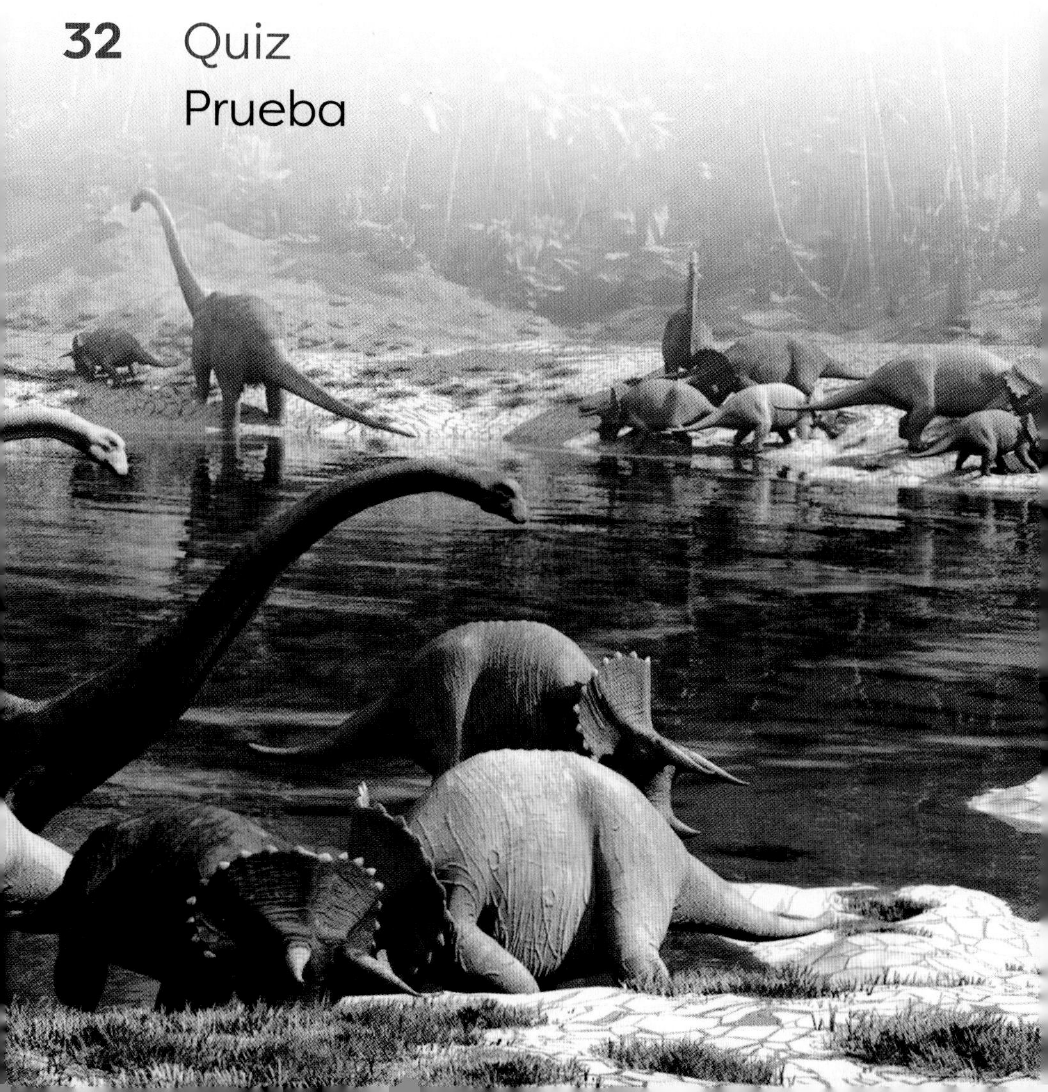

Meet the Triceratops
Conoce al Triceratops

I am a dinosaur.
I am big and strong.

Soy un dinosaurio.
Soy grande y fuerte.

frill
volante

I have horns on my head.
I have a bony frill
on my neck.

Tengo cuernos en la cabeza.
Tengo un volante óseo
en el cuello.

Triceratops
[try-SER-uh-tops]
Triceratops

I look fierce,
but I am gentle.
I spend all day
eating plants.
I snip off twigs and leaves
with my hard beak.

Me veo feroz,
pero soy manso.
Me paso el día
comiendo plantas.
Recorto ramas y hojas
con mi fuerte pico.

beak
pico

I live in a group called
a herd.
We look out for
hungry dinosaurs.
They might want to eat us!

Vivo en un grupo
llamado manada.
Estamos atentos por si
aparecen dinosaurios
hambrientos.
¡Podrían querer comernos!

Other dinosaurs live near the river with us.

Junto al río, con nosotros, viven otros dinosaurios.

Everything is quiet.
All of a sudden,
what do I see?

Todo está tranquilo.
De repente, ¿qué veo?

Watch Out for T. rex!
¡Cuidado con el T. rex!

The fiercest dinosaur of all!
He has short arms
with sharp claws.
He has a huge mouth
full of sharp teeth.

claws
garras

¡El dinosaurio más feroz
de todos!
Tiene brazos cortos
con garras afiladas.
Tiene una enorme boca
llena de dientes afilados.

Tyrannosaurus rex
[tie-RAN-uh-SORE-us]
Tiranosaurio rex

Another herd spots
T. rex, too. They run away
on their long legs.
They hide in the forest.

Otra manada también ve
al T. rex. Salen corriendo
con sus largas patas. Se
esconden en el bosque.

Ornithomimus
[OR-ni-thoh-MY-mus]

Ornitomimus

The duck-billed
dinosaurs stop eating.
They watch Tyrannosaurus.

Los dinosaurios de pico
de pato paran de comer.
Están pendientes del T. rex.

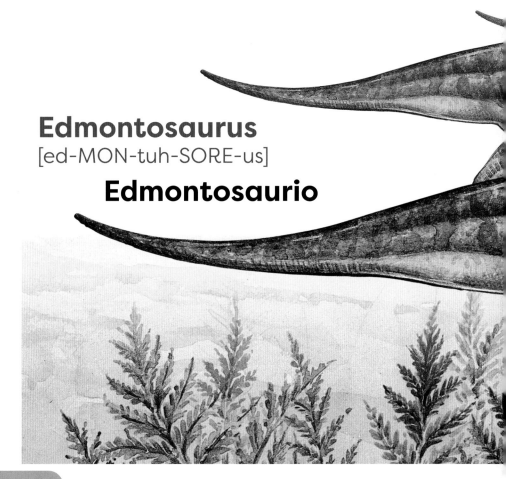

Edmontosaurus
[ed-MON-tuh-SORE-us]
Edmontosaurio

If he comes too close, they will run away.

bill
pico

Si se acerca mucho, saldrán corriendo.

The dinosaur with a big head sniffs the air.
He can smell T. rex.
He will also run away if T. rex comes too close.

El dinosaurio de la cabeza grande olfatea el aire.
Siente el olor del T. rex.
Él también saldrá corriendo si lo ve muy cerca.

Pachycephalosaurus
[PAK-ee-SEF-uh-low-SORE-us]
Paquicefalosaurio

The dinosaurs with head crests hoot in alarm.

Los dinosaurios de la cresta en la cabeza chillan alarmados.

Parasaurolophus
[par-uh-sore-OLL-uh-fuss]
Parasaurolofus

crest
cresta

Dinosaur in Danger
Un dinosaurio en peligro

I watch the other dinosaurs.
I forget to stay with
my herd.

Observo a los otros
dinosaurios.
Olvido quedarme cerca
de mi manada.

I can see T. rex.
He can see me.

Puedo ver al T. rex.
Él me puede ver a mí.

T. rex runs towards me.
He looks hungry.

El T. rex corre hacia mí.
Se ve hambriento.

teeth
dientes

His mouth is open. I can see
his sharp teeth.

Tiene la boca abierta.
Puedo ver sus dientes
afilados.

Thud! Thud!
¡Pum! ¡Pum!

He comes closer.

Se acerca.

He stands up.
He is very tall.
He lifts his head
and roars loudly.

Se endereza.
Es muy alto.
Levanta la cabeza
y lanza un fuerte
rugido.

He is trying to scare me.
But I am not scared.

Está tratando de asustarme,
pero yo no tengo miedo.

I lower my head.
I roar back.
I will try to scare him by
shaking my head and
showing off my big horns.

Yo bajo la cabeza.
También rujo.
Trataré de asustarlo
sacudiendo la cabeza
y mostrándole mis
grandes cuernos.

horns
cuernos

T. rex tries to bite
me with his
sharp teeth.
I am still
not scared.

El T. rex
trata de
morderme
con sus
afilados
dientes.
Yo sigo sin
sentir miedo.

I kick up the dust.
T. rex gives up
and walks away.

Levanto polvo con las patas.
El T. rex se rinde
y se aleja.

T. rex is getting tired.
He stops fighting.
Now I am safe.

El T. rex se está cansando.
Deja de luchar.
Ya estoy a salvo.

I am glad to be back
with my herd by the river.
The other dinosaurs come
back to the river too.
They eat quietly. I hope
T. rex won't come back again.

Me agrada estar de nuevo
con mi manada junto al río.
Los demás dinosaurios
también regresan al río.
Comen en silencio. Espero
que el T. rex no regrese.

Glossary
Glosario

beak
narrow, pointed end of Triceratops's mouth

claws
hard and sharp ends of T. rex's arms, used for slashing prey

crest
a body part that curved over some dinosaurs' heads

frill
a bony part of Triceratops's neck

horns
sharp points made from bone that stick out of some dinosaurs' heads

cresta
parte del cuerpo que se curvaba sobre la cabeza de algunos dinosaurios

cuernos
puntas afiladas hechas de hueso que sobresalían de la cabeza de algunos dinosaurios

garras
extremos duros y afilados de los brazos del T. rex que usaba para acuchillar a sus presas

pico
extremo delgado y puntiagudo de la boca del Triceratops

volante
parte ósea del cuello del Triceratops

Index
Índice

Quiz
Prueba

Answer the questions to see what you have learned. Check your answers with an adult.

1. What does Triceratops eat?
2. What is a group of dinosaurs called?
3. Which fierce dinosaur makes the other dinosaurs run away?
4. What does Triceratops use to fight T. rex?
5. Imagine if you were a dinosaur for a day. What would you eat? Would you have any special features?

1. Plants 2. A herd 3. Tyrannosaurus rex or T. rex 4. Its horns
5. Answers will vary

Responde las preguntas para saber cuánto aprendiste. Verifica tus respuestas con un adulto.

1. ¿Qué come el Triceratops?
2. ¿Cómo se llama un grupo de dinosaurios?
3. ¿Qué dinosaurio feroz hace huir a los otros dinosaurios?
4. ¿Qué usa el Triceratops para luchar contra el T. rex?
5. Imagina que eres un dinosaurio por un día. ¿Qué comerías? ¿Tendrías alguna característica especial?

1. Plantas 2. Una manada 3. El Tiranosaurio rex o T. rex 4. Sus cuernos
5. Las respuestas pueden variar.